MARK WILSON'S
Little Book of
Card Tricks

This book has been bound using
handcraft methods and Smyth-
sewn to ensure durability.

The dust jacket and interior
were designed by Terry Peterson,
using illustrations from
Mark Wilson's
Complete Course in Magic.

The text was edited by
Jason Rekulak.

The text was set in Didot,
Glypha, and Bureau Grotesque.

If you'd like to learn more about magic and take the next step in exploring our wonderful art, please write to me.

Happy Magic!

Mark Wilson

Mark Wilson
c/o Magic International
P.O. Box 801839
Santa Clarita, CA 91380-1839
www.markwilsonmagic.com

Card Flourishes

1

Fancy Flourishes with cards date far back to the self-styled "Kard Kings" of the vaudeville era. Houdini himself had lithographs showing him performing a myriad of masterful card flourishes.

One thing is certain — card flourishes are guaranteed to impress your audience. Whatever practice you give to such manipulations is time well spent. Your audience will recognize your skill and respect it.

One-Hand Cut

To many people, the sign of a real card expert is the ability to "cut" a pack of cards using only one hand. It appears difficult, but it's really much easier than it looks. Try it and you'll see!

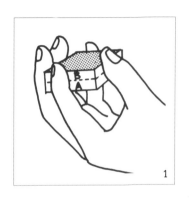

1. Hold the pack between the
tips of your thumb and fingers
as shown. Your first finger and

little finger are at the opposite
ends of the pack. Your other fingers and thumb are at the sides
as shown. Be sure your thumb
and fingers point almost straight
up. Also, hold the deck at the
tips of your fingers to form a
deep "well" between the deck
and the palm of your hand.

18

2. To begin, bend your thumb just enough to let the lower half (which we will call Packet A) of the deck drop into the palm of your cupped hand. The upper half remains held between the tips of your thumb and your two middle fingers. (We will call this Packet B.)

3. Bring your first finger below the lower half, Packet A, and push the packet upward, sliding it along the bottom card of the upper half, Packet B.

4. Continue pushing the edge of the lower half, Packet A, all the way up to your thumb as shown.

5. Now, gently extend your fingers just enough to allow the edges of the two halves to clear so that your thumb releases Packet B which drops to your curled finger.

6. By curling your first finger
lower into your hand, Packet B
will come down with it. Packet B
now becomes the lower half.

7. Slowly begin closing up your
hand—bringing both halves
together—with Packet A on top
of Packet B.

8. Extend your first finger around the pack. You have just done a one-hand cut!

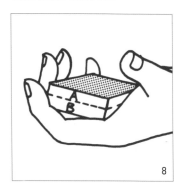

8

The One-Hand Fan

Though basically a card flourish, this is also a useful move in connection with various tricks. That makes two good reasons why you should practice it, as each will add a professional touch to your work.

1. Hold the pack in your right hand with your thumb on the face of the pack and your fingers flat

against the back. Position your thumb at the lower right-hand corner of the pack as shown.

2. Here is a view of the pack from the other side. Notice that your fingers only cover half of the length of the pack.

3. Now in one smooth continuous motion, start to slide your thumb upwards AT THE SAME TIME, curl your fingers inwards and downwards, as the pack begins to spread out in the form of a fan.

4. Continue sliding your thumb upwards as the fingers continue pushing the cards in a sort of "smearing" motion down the heel of the hand until they curl into the palm—almost forming a fist with the cards held tightly between. When your thumb and fingers

have reached this position, the fan
should be fully formed as shown.

5. Your fingers are responsible
for forming the lower half of the
fan and the thumb is responsible
for forming the upper half. Do
not be disappointed if you cannot master the one-hand fan

immediately. Careful practice
will teach you exactly how much
pressure to exert with the thumb
and fingers in order for the
cards to distribute properly from
the top and bottom of the pack,
forming an evenly spaced fan.

6. Here is a view of the completed
fan from the other side. Notice
the right fingers have curled
into the palm of the hand to
form a fist.

Automatic Card Discovery

2

EFFECT

Perhaps one of the most puzzling of all card effects is when a magician causes a selected card to reverse itself and appear face up among the face-down cards in the deck. Here is one of the most basic and yet most effective means of accomplishing this feat.

SECRET AND
PREPARATION

A The trick depends upon having the bottom card of the deck reversed from the start. This can be set up beforehand, or it can be executed easily when the spectators' eyes leave your hands.

B With the deck resting face up across the fingers of your left hand, your right thumb and fingers grip the ends of the pack from below, as shown. Slide the

pack toward the tips of the left
fingers, at the same time tilting
or rotating the deck up on its left
edge. This leaves the lone card—
in this case the eight of spades—
still resting on the left fingers.

C Continue the rotary motion
until the right hand has turned
the pack face down on the eight
of spades, which thus, without

the spectators knowing it, has become a face-up card at the bottom of the pack. You are now ready to present the trick.

METHOD

1. Spread the cards in your hands face down so that a spectator has an opportunity to freely select any card from the deck. Care must be taken here not to spread the cards too near the bottom of the deck, to avoid accidentally flashing the face-up bottom card.

2. As soon as the card is selected by the spectator, square up the deck in your left hand and ask the spectator to look at the card.

3. At the moment when the spectator's eyes are focusing on the card, the left hand turns completely over and sets the deck of cards on the table. This action turns all of the cards in the deck face up, except

for the "bottom" card which is now
face down. Because of this single
reversed card, it appears that the
deck is still face down.

4. Leave the deck sitting on the
table, as you tell the spectator
to show the card to spectators.

5. When the spectator has shown
the card, pick up the deck, in its
secretly reversed position, with
your left hand. Particular care
must be taken here to keep the
deck squared up so as not to

flash the face-up pack below
the top, single reversed card.

6. Holding the deck firmly, ask
the spectator to push the card
face down anywhere in the deck.
Unknown to the spectator, the
card is really being put into a face-
up deck. (Except for the top card.)

7. When the spectator has inserted the card into the deck, place the deck behind your back and explain that since the spectator touched only one card in the deck, that card will be a bit warmer than the other cards. State that, due to your highly trained sense of touch, you will be able to find the card and reveal it in a startling way.

8. When you place the deck behind your back, simply turn over the single reversed card and

replace it face up on the deck. Now, every card in the deck is facing the same direction, *except* the spectator's card.

Super Automatic Card Discovery

In performing the **Automatic Card Discovery**, here is another very easy and clever method for reversing the bottom card and secretly turning over the pack.

METHOD

1. It is not necessary to have the bottom card reversed before the start of the trick.

2. After the spectator has selected his card from the deck, tell him to remember the card and that, after he replaces it in the deck, you are going to place the deck behind your back and locate his card in a very startling fashion...*at which time you DEMONSTRATE what you are going to do.*

3. Place the deck behind your back. Turn the bottom card face up. Then turn the whole pack over so that it is all face up except for the one face-down card on top.

4. Bring the deck out from behind your *back. You are now ready for the spectator to replace his card in the pack.*

COMMENTS AND SUGGESTIONS

With this method, you can perform the trick at any time with no previous "set-up." The spectator may even shuffle the deck himself before he freely selects a card. It only takes a moment to set up the pack behind your back as you "demonstrate" the first part of the startling way in which you are going to find the spectator's card. However, when you do this "demonstration," do not tell him that his card will later be discovered face-up in a face-down pack, or you may alert spectators to your secret.

This method not only allows you to reverse the bottom card, but also to turn the pack over for the replacement of the selected card without any tricky moves whatsoever. When you first place the deck behind your back, just do it naturally, as if you were illustrating what is going to happen next. You can now present a very puzzling, self-working card trick that appears to require great skill yet is practically automatic in every respect.

Fantastic Five

3

EFFECT

This is a clever, self-working card discovery utilizing a prepared deck in its simplest form. The trick finishes with a double twist that will leave the onlookers completely baffled. Adding one surprise onto another is always a good policy, especially with card tricks.

A card is freely selected

by a spectator and returned to the top of the deck. The pack is then given a cut. You spread the pack on the table, revealing that one card is face up. It is a five. You explain that the face-up card, the five, is your magical indicator. Then you count down five cards in the deck below where the face-up card chosen was located. Turning up the fifth card, it proves to be

the card chosen by the
spectator! If that were not
enough, you now turn
the four cards that were
between the face-up card
and the spectator's card.
All four are aces!

SECRET AND
PREPARATION

To prepare, run through
the pack and remove the
four aces and any five-
card. Square up the pack

and place the five face up on the bottom of the face-down pack. Place the four aces face down below the five.

A The first illustration shows the proper preparation with the pack held face up.

B This shows the pack held in its normal face-down position. Square up the pack and you're ready to begin.

METHOD

1. Spread the pack and invite a
spectator to select a card. Be
sure not to spread the pack too
near the bottom, thereby accidentally exposing the face-up
five.

2. Tell the spectator to be sure to remember the card. Square up the deck and place it on the table.

3. Ask the spectator to place the card on top of the deck.

4. Have the spectator cut the deck.

5. Let the spectator complete
the cut.

NOTE: *Unknown to the spectator,
when the deck is cut, the four aces
and the face-up five are placed
directly above the selected card.*

6. Explain to the spectator that

something magical is going to
happen. At the same time,
spread the deck to the one face-
up card in the deck.

7. Separate all the cards to the
right of the face-up five.

8. Explain that the face-up card
is your magical indicator card
and that it will help to locate

the card the spectator selected.
Since the card is a five, that
must be a clue. Count down
five cards in the deck.

9. Push the five, the four face-
down aces below it, and the next
card (the spectator's card) all
forward from the pack.

10. Turn over the fifth card and

show it to be the card that the
spectator selected.

11. The spectator will assume
that the trick is over. Not content
with this, you turn over the four
remaining cards to reveal the
four aces. This second, added
surprise, the appearance of the
aces, adds greatly to the effect.
This is also a good lead-in to
any four-ace trick.

COMMENTS AND
SUGGESTIONS

Here is another presentation idea.
After the spectator has returned
his selected card to the pack and
completed the cut, pick up the
deck and give it a snap before you
spread it along the table. Say that
this will cause a card to turn over
somewhere in the deck. When
the spread reveals the face-up
Five, count down to the chosen
card. Turn it over, revealing it to
be the spectator's selected card.

Now for the added touch: you then gather up the upper and lower portions of the pack, *placing the "Aces" half of the deck in TOP*. Say, "Whenever I snap the pack a second time, something good always turn up"...SNAP!... "like the four Aces!" Then deal the four Aces from the top of the deck, turning each Ace face up as you place it on the table.

Turnover Card

4

This surprising effect is performed with a pack of ordinary playing cards. It can be done with a borrowed deck and requires no skill or practice. The trick depends on the use of a key card, which is one of the most basic and simple methods used in card magic to locate a selected card in a pack of cards.

EFFECT

You have a spectator shuffle a pack of cards and cut the cards anywhere the spectator wishes. Tell the spectator to look at the card that was cut to and then complete the cut, thus burying the card in the deck. At this point, you take the cards in your hands for the first time and proceed to find the selected card.

SECRET AND PREPARATION

The secret of the trick depends entirely upon the performer secretly learning the bottom card of the pack before it is placed on the table to begin the trick. This card is called a key card because it will be your key to the location of the select-ed card. In the following description, we will assume that your key card (the card

on the bottom of the deck)
is the two of clubs.

METHOD

1. If you use a pack of cards that
is already in its case at the start,
you can glimpse the bottom card
as you remove the cards from the
case. Just lay the pack face down
and go right into the trick without a shuffle.

2. Even better, if people want to
shuffle the pack, let them. Often

when a spectator is squaring up the pack after shuffling, he will flash the bottom card in your direction, not realizing it has anything to do with the trick.

3. If you don't get a glimpse of the card during the shuffle, pick up the pack in your hands, turn it face up, and begin running the cards from hand to hand, as shown.

Comment that the cards appear
to be well-shuffled, and it would
be impossible for you to know
their order. Of course, here you
see and remember your key
card. Lay the pack face down
on the table and you're ready
to make magic happen.

Mark Wilson's
Little Book of
Card Tricks

Running Press
PHILADELPHIA • LONDON

A Running Press ® Miniature Edition™
Copyright © 2000 by Mark Wilson
All rights reserved under the Pan-American and International
Copyright Conventions
Printed in China

Library of Congress Cataloging-in-Publication Number 00-133408

Front Cover Art courtesy of U.S. Playing Card Company
Back Cover Art and photograph on page 55: © 2000 Michael Weiss

ISBN-13: 978-0-7624-0834-4
ISBN-10: 0-7624-0834-0

This book may be ordered by mail from the publisher.
Please include $1.00 for postage and handling.
But try your bookstore first!

Running Press Book Publishers
125 South Twenty-second Street
Philadelphia, Pennsylvania 19103-4399

Visit us on the web!
www.runningpress.com

contents

Introduction

Welcome to my wonderful world of Magic. You're about to enter a mysterious and fascinating realm in which you'll learn some truly baffling illusions.

For most of the tricks in this book, you'll find detailed information on:

• **EFFECT**—what the spectator

will see; the mystery or miracle, as performed by you, the magician.

• **SECRET AND PREPARA-TION** — the props you'll need, and the secret of how tricks work.

• **METHOD** — clearly illustrated, step-by-step instructions on how to present tricks to an audience.

• **COMMENTS AND SUGGES-TIONS** — extra tips and ideas that will help you make tricks even more amazing and entertaining.

The secrets to good magic tricks are quite simple. So don't judge a magic trick by its secret—judge it by its effect on the audience. To ensure a captivating effect, it's important that you remember these rules whenever you perform:

• **NEVER REVEAL THE SECRET**. If you reveal how a trick is done, the mystery, the excitement, and the magic are gone and the entertainment value lost.

• **NEVER REPEAT A TRICK FOR THE SAME AUDIENCE.** When you do a magic trick for the same audience a second time, they will know what to expect and they will be more likely to "catch on" to the secret.

• **ALWAYS PRACTICE BEFORE YOU PERFORM.** By taking the time necessary to rehearse tricks, you will build self-confidence, which will dramatically enhance your performance before an audience.

As a magician, you'll appear to make the impossible happen. There aren't many people who can pull this off. So practice and perform your magic well, and you'll make the magic fun for yourself and a rare treat for your audience!

4. With the pack lying face down on the table and the audience satisfied that the cards are well mixed, ask a spectator to divide the pack into two parts.

5. Tell the spectator to cut anywhere in the deck and to place the upper portion on the table.

NOTE: *The card that the spectator has cut to, which will be the selected card, is marked with an X in the illustrations to make it easier for you to follow.*

6. After the cards have been cut, tell the spectator to remove the top card of the lower half, look at it, remember it, and place it on top of the other half of the pack. Let's assume that the card is the five of diamonds.

7. Point to the lower half and ask the spectator to put those cards on top of the selected card so that it will be buried somewhere in the pack.

NOTE: *In placing the lower half*

on top of the upper half the spectator is also placing your key card directly above the chosen card. Ask the spectator to give the pack another complete cut and then to let someone else cut it also.

Spectator Looks At Card

8. When this is done, take the

pack and begin dealing cards
one by one on the table, turning
each card face up. Announce
that you are trying to get an
impression of the selected card,
but that the spectator is not to
say anything, even if the selected
card appears, or you will have
to begin all over.

Key Card

9

Selected Card

10

9. As you deal cards one at a time from the pack, turn each face up, watch for your key card, the two of clubs. When it shows up, deal it on the table along with the others. You now know that the next card will be the spectator's card (the five of diamonds).

10. Deal the next card, the five of diamonds, but instead of stopping, just continue dealing as if you haven't reached the chosen card.

11. After you have dealt several more cards, tell the spectator you have received an impression. Say, "The next card I turn over will be your card." The spectator will probably say you are wrong.

12. But instead of dealing the next card off the pack, reach among the face-up cards on the table and draw out the five of diamonds.

13. Turn over the five and explain, "I said the next card I turned over would be yours—and it is!"

NOTE: *When you deal past the selected card, the spectator is sure that the trick has gone wrong. But when you actually do turn the selected card face down, you really prove your magical powers!*

Double
Mystery
X

EFFECT

Two spectators are invit-
ed to assist you. You
give the spectator on your
left a pack of cards and a
pen and ask that spectator
to place the pack behind
their back and mark an X
across the FACE of any
card with a pen. You give
the same deck and pen to
the spectator on your right
and ask that spectator to
mark the BACK of any

card, with the pack behind
the spectator. You return
the deck to the spectator
on your left and ask that
spectator to run through
the deck and find the card
with the X on the FACE,
remove it and hold it
between both hands so
that it is out of sight. This
done, the spectator on the
right is again given the
deck and asked to find
their card, the one with the
X on the BACK. On search-

ing through the deck, the spectator on the right finds that the card is missing. When the spectator on the left turns the card over, it is found to have an X on the BACK. It appears as if both spectators have chosen and marked the same card!

SECRET AND PREPARATION

The secret to this "coincidence" is so simple it's surprising. It all depends upon the fact that the pen that you give to the spectators just doesn't work. For best results, use a pen with a felt tip. All that is required is to let it sit without the cap on until the tip is dried out. If a pencil is used, it is necessary to dip the top of the pencil in clear varnish and allow it to dry overnight. This will pre-

vent the pencil from mak-
ing a mark on the cards,
although it appears to
have a perfectly good
point.

To prepare, remove any
card from the pack and
mark an X on both sides
with a pen or pencil that
really works and matches
the special one you will
use in the trick. The lines
that form the X should
appear irregular, as if the

mark were made behind the back. Place the card back in the deck, and you're ready.

METHOD

1. With two spectators to assist you, give the deck, face up, to the spectator on your left. Ask this spectator to place the deck behind their back, to run through the cards, and without looking at it, to bring any card to the top of the deck.

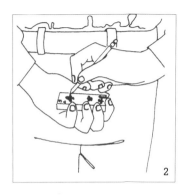

2. When this has been done, give
the spectator the prepared pen
and instruct the spectator to

mark an X across the face of the
card and then return the pen to
you. Ask the spectator to mix the
cards behind their back so the
marked card is lost somewhere
in the deck. Have the spectator
hand you the deck.

3. Turn the deck face down and
hand it to the spectator on your
right. Instruct the second spectator just as you did the first spectator. But tell this spectator to
mark an X on the back of any
card and mix the cards.

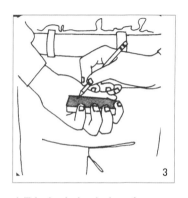

3

4. Take back the deck and put the pen away. Give the deck again to the spectator on your

left, and ask this spectator to
look through the cards face up
and remove the card the specta-

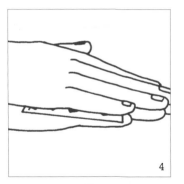

4

tor marked from the deck. Have the spectator hold this card between the palms of the hands so no one else can see the card.

NOTE: *Because of the prepared pen, neither spectator has made a mark on any card, and both are unaware of the prepared X card in the deck.*

5. Give the deck to the spectator on your right and ask this spectator to do the same: "Please run through the deck and remove

your card, the one with the X on the back." Of course, the spectator will be unable to find the card.

6. After several attempts, call attention to the fact that the only card missing from the deck is the one that the other spectator is holding. Tell the spectator on your left to look at the back of the card. It appears that the two spectators were somehow able to freely select and mark the very same card in the deck.

COMMENTS AND SUGGESTIONS

It is a good idea at the start of the trick to run through the cards face up and show them to be an ordinary deck. In order to do this, it is necessary to have the secret X close to the bottom of the deck. Then, run through the cards face up, supposedly to show that they are all different. Just be careful not to spread the cards near the position in the deck where the X card is located.

The spectator will believe everything is on the up-and-up. You will be amazed at the effect that this trick has, as there appears to be no reasonable explanation to the astonishing results. Properly performed, no one will ever suspect the special pen is the secret to the mystery.

Super Double X Mystery

One very subtle convincer, which can make the trick a **COMPLETE** baffler, is to introduce a duplicate pen (the one that **REALLY** made the X on the card), after the prepared pen has done the dirty work. Simply have the duplicate in your pocket, and after the second spectator has made his "mark," casually place the pen in the pocket with the duplicate. As the second spectator is looking for the card with the X, remove the unprepared pen and "help" him search by pointing to various parts of the deck with the "real" pen. Then just lay the pen somewhere in plain sight. Now *everything* can be examined.

Super Anytime Double X Mystery

With this method, you can perform the Double X Mystery at any time during your card routine...

even though the deck has been used for a number of other tricks and even examined by the audience!

SECRET AND PREPARATION

Before the show, place the X marked card either (A) under your belt behind your back or (B) in a "gimmick" card holder made from a safety pin

A

B

C

and a paper clip. The special card is placed in the paper clip and the "holder" pinned inside the back of your coat (C) so that the card is just hidden by the bottom edge of your coat.

METHOD

1. Have a spectators shuffle the deck. Then, place the deck behind your back to illustrate to your two assistants what they are to do— *now secretly add the X card to the deck!* Now proceed with the Super Double X Mystery just as described.

You Do
As I Do

6

EFFECT

Two packs of cards are thoroughly shuffled. One is shuffled by a spectator, and you shuffle the other pack. You and the spectator then exchange packs, and each selects a card, taking care that the other person does not see it. The cards are both replaced in their decks. You and the spectator exchange decks again,

and each finds the dupli-
cate of the card selected
in the other pack. You
and the spectator then
place the selected cards
face down on the table.
When the two cards are
turned up, they prove
to be identical.

SECRET AND PREPARATION

This is one of the finest
self-working tricks in card

magic. You need only two ordinary decks of cards. The trick can be performed anytime, anywhere, with no previous preparation. Let's assume that one deck has red backs and the other blue.

METHOD

1. Place both decks on the table and ask the spectator to select either one. This is a free choice. Let's assume that the spectator

takes the deck with the red
backs. This leaves you with the
blue-backed deck.

2. Tell the spectator to "do as
I do." Shuffle your blue deck,
and the spectator should do the
same with the red deck.

3. As you complete the last shuffle, square up your deck, as
shown in the picture. As you
do, turn the deck on its edge,
glimpse the bottom card, and
remember it. Do not call atten-

tion to this, just remember the bottom card, as it will serve as your key card for the rest of the trick.

NOTE: *In the illustration, the eight of diamonds is your key card.*

4. Stress to the spectator that, to

make sure that all is fair, you will trade decks, so you will be using a deck that the spectator personally has shuffled. Exchange decks with the spectator. Unknown to the spectator, you know the bottom card of the blue deck the spectator now holds.

5. Instruct the spectator to fan open the blue deck, holding the deck up, so that you cannot see the faces, just as you are doing with the red deck. The spectator is to freely select any card from

Magician

5

Spectator

5

the deck, and you will do likewise.
Tell the spectator it's best if the
spectator selects a favorite card,
and that you will do the same
and select your favorite card.

NOTE: *To make the illustrations
easy to follow, we have marked
the spectator's card with an X.*

Magician   6

Spectator   6

Magician   7

Spectator   7

6. Ask the spectator to place the
selected card on the top of the
deck, as shown, as you do the

same with your card. It is not necessary for you to remember the card that you have selected at this point. Just remember your key card, the one that is on the bottom of the deck now held by the spectator—the eight of diamonds.

7. Have the spectator square up the cards, as you do the same. Each of you places your deck on the table.

8. Tell the spectator to cut the deck, as you cut your deck, thus

burying the selected cards somewhere in the middle of each pack. Unknown to the spectator, this cut places the bottom card, which is your key card (the eight of diamonds), directly above the spectator's card.

9. Have the spectator complete the cut and ask the spectator to cut two more times, as you do the same. Be sure that each cut is a

single cut and that the cut is completed each time. No matter how many times you cut the deck, as long as each cut is completed before the next cut is started, the key card will stay next to the selected card.

10. Stress the fact that there's no possible way that you could know where the spectator's favorite card is now located in the deck, and, likewise the spectator could not know where your card is.

11. Trade decks with the spectator once more. You now hold the one you originally shuffled, the blue deck with your key card.

12. Have the spectator look through the red deck and remove the card which matches the spectator's favorite card, and you will do the same with the blue deck.

Key Card Spectator's Card

13

14

13. While the spectator does this, you spread your deck until you locate your key card, the eight of diamonds. The card immediately to the right of the key card will be the card the spectator selected.

14. Tell the spectator to remove

the selected card without showing its face, and you will do the
same. Actually, you remove the
card which you now know to be
the one the spectator selected,
the two of clubs.

15. Have the spectator place the
card on the table, and you place
yours beside it.

16. Say, "It would be quite a
coincidence if we both had the
same favorite card, wouldn't it?"
Again, stress the fact that you

each have been doing the same
thing: YOU DO AS I DO. You
and the spectator turn your
cards face up at the same time.
The spectator will be amazed
to see that the cards match!

The Signed
Card in Wallet

7

Here is an effect which will cause spectators to give you credit for remarkable skill, yet no special moves or long practice is required. Misdirection is the main factor and even that becomes almost automatic, if you follow this timely, well-paced routine that has been carefully designed to baffle the sharpest spectators.

EFFECT

A card is selected by a
spectator who signs his
name on the back. The
magician brings out his
wallet which contains a
"prediction" card which
he has signed. When the
"prediction" card is
revealed, it is found to
match the spectator's
selection.

SECRET AND PREPARATION

For this trick you need a few simple props. First, an ordinary book-style wallet or checkbook. You will also need a pen, a small piece of "double-faced" cellophane tape and a deck of cards. Also, you will need one duplicate card from another deck. It can be any card you choose, but for our explanation we will use an extra Four of Hearts. This card, known as the "prediction card," can be taken from a pack of a totally different design.

METHOD

1. Open the wallet or checkbook flat and place it on the table as shown. Next, sign your name across the back of the duplicate Four of Hearts and place it FACE DOWN on the LEFT

SIDE of the wallet. *Now fold over the right side,* enclosing the card inside the wallet.

2. Turn the entire wallet over and place a small (1½ -inch) piece of double-faced cellophane tape in the center of this side of the wallet. Then turn the wallet back

over to its original position. Be careful not to stick the tape to the table.

3. With the taped side toward your body, insert the wallet in your left inside coat pocket.

Four of Hearts

4. Place the pen

in the same pocket. Look
through the deck until you
locate the Four of Hearts. (This
has been marked with an "X"
in the illustrations.) Remove the
Four and place it on top of the
deck. You are ready to perform
a truly fantastic trick.

5. Spread the deck face down
from hand to hand and ask a
spectator to just TOUCH a card.
*Emphasize that he has a completely
free choice of ANY card.*

6. When he does, separate the pack ABOVE the card (Here marked with a "Z") that the spectator touched. Keep his "selected" card (Z) at the top of the left half of the pack.

7. Deal this

selected card (Z), *without looking*
at it on top of the cards held in
the right hand, explaining that
you will move the chosen card to
the top of the deck.

8. Now, place the right-hand
packet of cards on top of those
in the left hand and square the
cards up. *You should now have the
selected card (Z) on top of the deck,
with the Four of Hearts (X) directly
below it.*

9. Hold the deck in your left

hand. With your
right hand,
bring the wallet
from your
inside coat
pocket. Handle
it in a casual
manner, keeping
the taped side
toward you.

10. Then, tilt the
top (upper end)
of the wallet
toward your

body, so the taped side is underneath. With your right hand, place the wallet squarely on top of the pack in the left hand.

11. Hold the wallet against the deck with your left thumb while your right hand moves back toward the pocket for the pen. With your thumb, press firmly on the wallet causing the top card (Z) to stick to the tape on the underside of the wallet.

12. With your right hand, remove the pen from your pocket and hand to the spectator.

13. **NOTE:** *Reaching back into your pocket supplies a perfect reason for momentarily leaving the wallet on the deck as a resting place as you bring out the pen to give to the spectator.*

14. With your right hand, remove the wallet from the top of the deck to the table, secretly carrying away the spectator's card (Z)

with it. *The spectator thinks his selected card is still on top of the deck, but really the Four of Hearts is in its place.*

15. Deal the top card, NOW THE FOUR OF HEARTS, onto the table, face down, to the left

Card with
your name

16

17

of the wallet. State, "I'd like you
to sign your name across the
back of your card to clearly
identify your selection."

16. Have the spectator sign the
back of the tabled card (which
only you know is the Four of

Hearts). When he is finished, replace the pen in your coat pocket.

17. Open the wallet to reveal your signed, face-down "prediction card." Remove the card from the wallet and place it, still face down, on the table next to the spectator's card.

18. *Pick up the wallet and place it back in your coat pocket thus getting rid of any evidence beforehand. Be sure to handle the wallet*

so as not to reveal (or unstick) the card held on to the underneath side.

19. Before turning the two cards over, pause a moment to tell your audience about the "Mysteries of ESP," thus building up the suspense a little before you turn both signed cards face up. Of course, your "prediction" proves to be correct making the mystery complete!

COMMENTS AND SUGGESTIONS

This is a VERY STRONG mental effect in which no manipulative skill is involved. It should be presented in your own personal style.

NOTE: *Some coats have the inside pocket on the right side, not the left. In that case, after placing the "touched" card on the top of the pack, transfer the pack from your*

*left hand to your right. Then
remove the wallet with your left
hand and place it on top of the
pack in your right hand. The proce-
dure is then exactly the same.*

COMMENTS AND SUGGESTIONS

This feat of card magic
was originated by the late
Paul Le Paul and used for
many years. It creates a
startling effect, that is one
of the best in magic. Give
this the practice it
deserves and you will
have a card effect that will
entertain and mystify all
who witness it.